How I Live in Christ

written & illustrated by Darcy Jackson

How I Live In Christ
Copyright © 2023 Darcy Jackson (DarcyL)
All rights reserved.
ISBN: 978-1-990871-122

Published by Fictitious Ink Publishing, Tumbler Ridge,
BC, Canada, V0C 2W0

Scripture quotations are taken from the Holy Bible,
New International Version®, NIV®. Copyright ©
1973, 1978, 1984, 2011 by Biblica, Inc.™ Used by
permission of Zondervan. All rights reserved world-
wide. www.zondervan.com The "NIV" and "New
International Version" are trademarks registered in the
United States Patent and Trademark Office by Biblica,
Inc.™

This booklet is devoted to
Lord Jesus Christ
and dedicated to
Pam, my friend
and sister in Christ.
I hope these words
multiply your faith!
I love you,
DarcyL
❤️

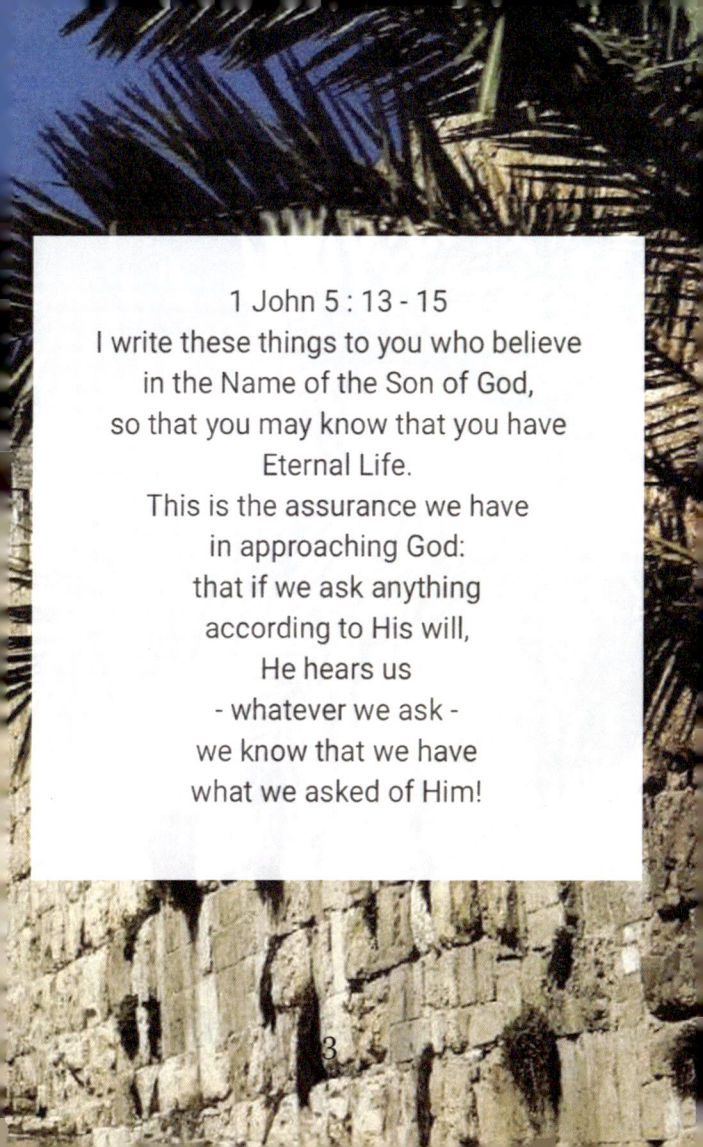

1 John 5 : 13 - 15
I write these things to you who believe
in the Name of the Son of God,
so that you may know that you have
Eternal Life.
This is the assurance we have
in approaching God:
that if we ask anything
according to His will,
He hears us
- whatever we ask -
we know that we have
what we asked of Him!

A

ASK

Mathew 7 : 7
"Ask and it will be given to you. Seek and you will find. Knock and the door will be opened to you".

Ask
Seek
Knock

4

I ask You to be with me Lord.
I seek Your presence.

B

BELIEVE

John 14:11
"Believe Me when I say that
I AM in the Father and the
Father is in Me. Or at least
believe on the evidence of the
miracles themselves".

I believe You Jesus and I believe _in_ You!

Jesus said, "If a man is thirsty,
let him come to me & drink.
Whoever believes in Me,
as Scripture has said,
streams of living Water
will flow from
within him."

C

CONFESS

Romans 10 : 9
If you confess with your
mouth, "Jesus is Lord",
and believe in your
heart that God raised
Him from the dead,
you will be saved.

*Jesus
is
Lord*

D

DIE to sins

1 Peter 2 : 24
He Himself bore our sins
in His body on the tree, so
that we might die to sins
and live for righteousness

I die to sin and live for righteousness.

E

ENCOURAGE

Hebrews 3 : 13
Encourage one another daily,
as long as it is called Today,
so that none of you may be
hardened by sin's deceitfulness

*I encourage all
to grow strong
in the Lord Jesus*

F

FORGIVE

Colossians 3 : 13
Bear with each other and
forgive whatever grievances
you may have
against one another. Forgive
as the Lord forgave you.

I forgive, as the
Lord has forgiven me

15

G

GIVE

Luke 6 : 38
Give, and it will be given
to you. A good measure;
pressed down, shaken
together and running
over, will be poured into
your lap.

*I give generously
because the Lord
has given to me
in abundance!*

H

HUMBLE

1 Peter 5 : 6
Humble yourselves under
God's mighty hand, that He
may lift you up in due time.

God opposes the proud but gives grace to the humble.

I
IMITATE

Ephesians 5 : 1, 2
Be imitators of God, as dearly
loved children. Live
a life of love, just as Christ loved
us and gave Himself up for us as
a fragrant offering and sacrifice
to God.

I ponder how to imitate Christ.

J

JUDGE not

Luke 6 : 37
Do not judge, and you will not be
judged. Do not condemn, and you
will not be condemned. Forgive
and you will be forgiven.

Lord Jesus,
when I remember Your
compassion towards me,
I can resist the temptation
to judge others.

K

KNOCK

Matthew 7 : 8
Everyone who asks, receives.
He who seeks, finds. And to
him who knocks, the door will
be opened.

*I'm knocking on
Heaven's door.*

L

LIVE by faith

Galatians 2 : 20b
The life I live in the body,
I live by faith in the Son of
God, who loved me and
gave Himself for me.

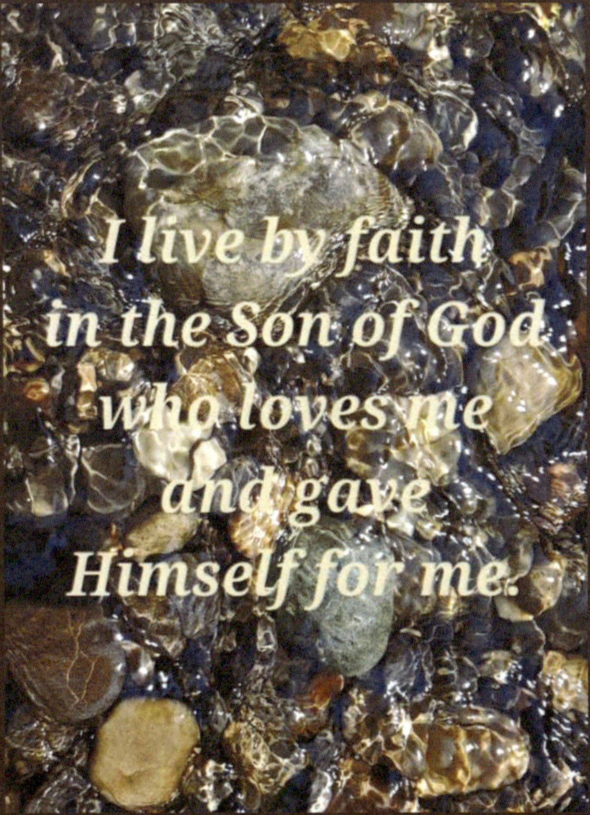

I live by faith
in the Son of God
who loves me
and gave
Himself for me.

M

MEDITATE

Psalm 48 : 9
Within Your temple, O God,
we meditate on Your unfailing
love. Like Your Name, O God,
Your praise reaches to the ends
of the earth.

*In Your temple, I meditate
on Your unfailing love.*

N

NUMBER

Psalm 90 : 12
Teach us to number our
days aright, that we
may gain a heart of
wisdom.

Lord, I know my days are numbered.
I hold each day as sacred and precious.
Thank You.

O

OFFER

Hebrews 13 : 15
Through Jesus, let us
continually offer to God
a sacrifice of praise -
the fruit of lips that
confess His Name.

Offer a sacrifice of
PRAISE

Praise Him! Praise Him!

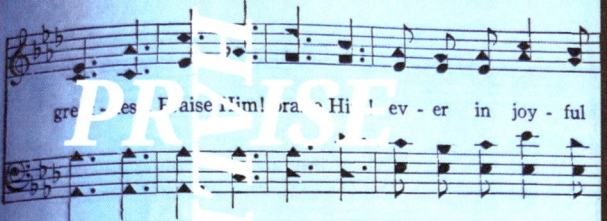

gre... ...es ...Praise Him! ...ra..se Hi... ev - er   in   joy - ful

Praise the Lord

(Perez)

*"Praise ye the Lord. Praise ye the Lord from the heavens:
Praise him in the heights. Praise ye him,
all his angels."—Ps. 148; 1, 2*

J. Kempthorne

1. Praise the Lord, ye heav'ns, a-dore Him! Praise Him, an - gels,
2. Praise the Lord for He hath spo-ken; Worlds His might-y
3. Praise the Lord for He is glo-rious; Nev - er shall His
4. Praise the God of our sal - va-tion; Hosts on high, His

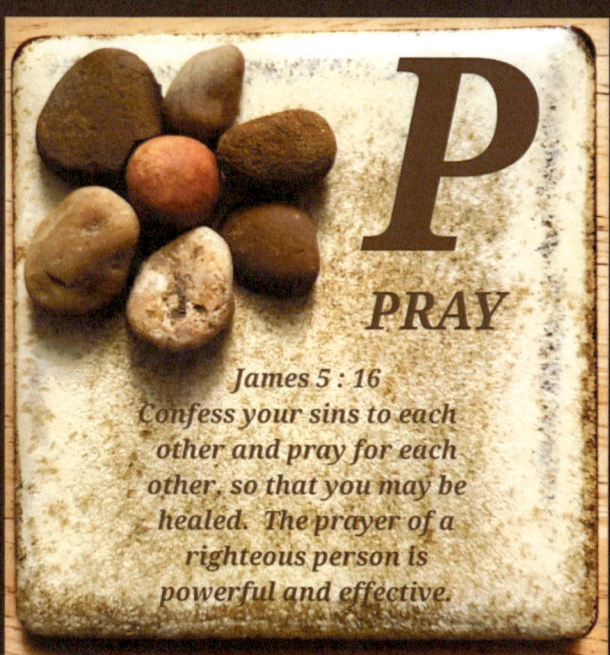

P

PRAY

James 5 : 16
Confess your sins to each other and pray for each other, so that you may be healed. The prayer of a righteous person is powerful and effective.

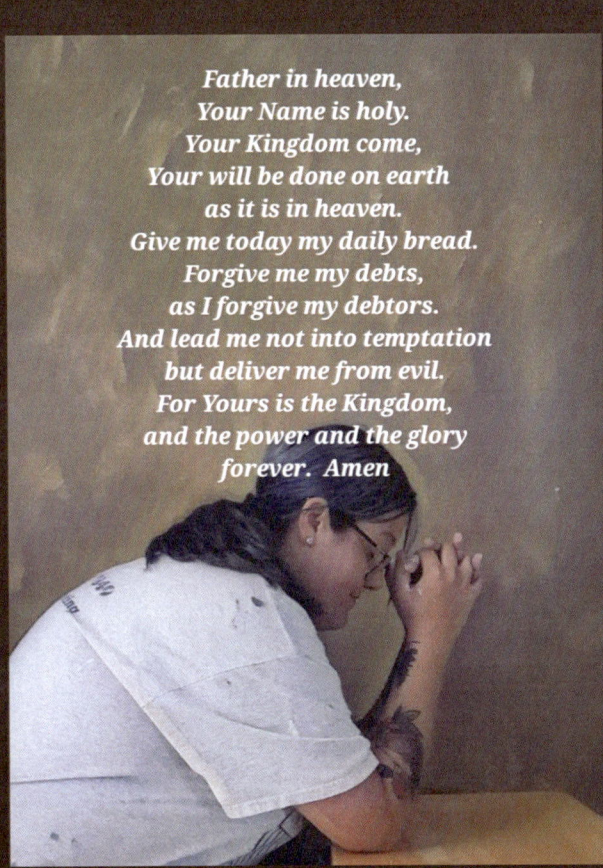

Father in heaven,
Your Name is holy.
Your Kingdom come,
Your will be done on earth
as it is in heaven.
Give me today my daily bread.
Forgive me my debts,
as I forgive my debtors.
And lead me not into temptation
but deliver me from evil.
For Yours is the Kingdom,
and the power and the glory
forever. Amen

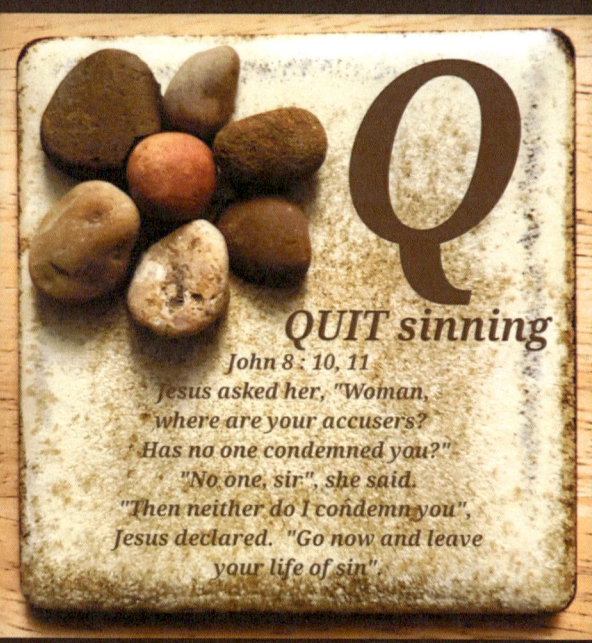

Q

QUIT sinning

John 8 : 10, 11
Jesus asked her, "Woman,
where are your accusers?
Has no one condemned you?"
"No one, sir", she said.
"Then neither do I condemn you",
Jesus declared. "Go now and leave
your life of sin".

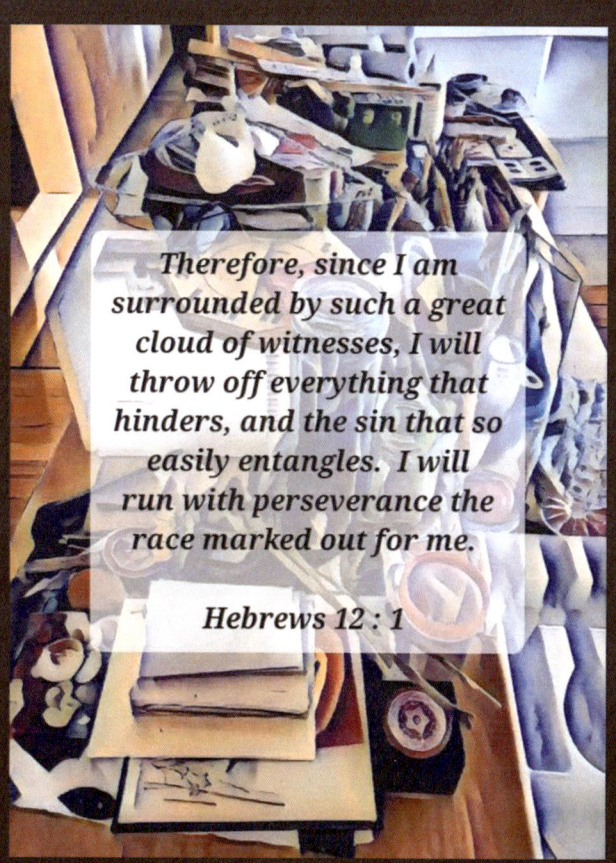

> *Therefore, since I am surrounded by such a great cloud of witnesses, I will throw off everything that hinders, and the sin that so easily entangles. I will run with perseverance the race marked out for me.*
>
> *Hebrews 12 : 1*

R

REPENT

Acts 2 : 38
Peter replied, "Repent and be baptized, everyone of you, in the Name of Jesus Christ, so that your sins may be forgiven. And you will receive the gift of the Holy Spirit. The promise is for you and your children and for all who are far off.

Lord Jesus;
I repent and I make a complete
180° turn around in my life.
Amen

S

SERVE

1 Peter 4 : 8 - 10
Above all, love each other deeply, because love covers over a multitude of sins. Offer hospitality without grumbling. Each one should use whatever gift he has received, to serve others....

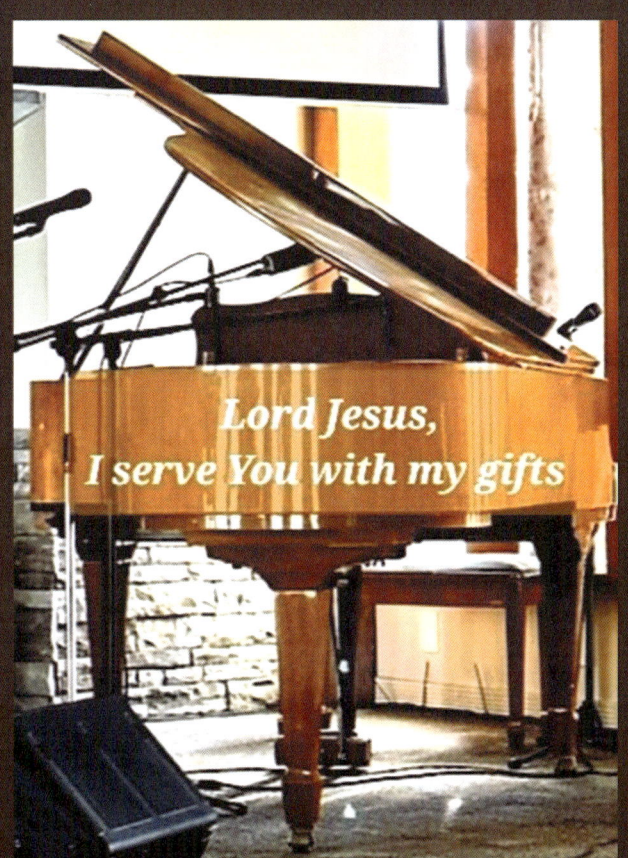

Lord Jesus,
I serve You with my gifts

T

TRUST

John 14 : 1
"Do not let your hearts be
troubled. You trust in God;
trust also in Me".

TRUST

TRUST IN THE LORD

43

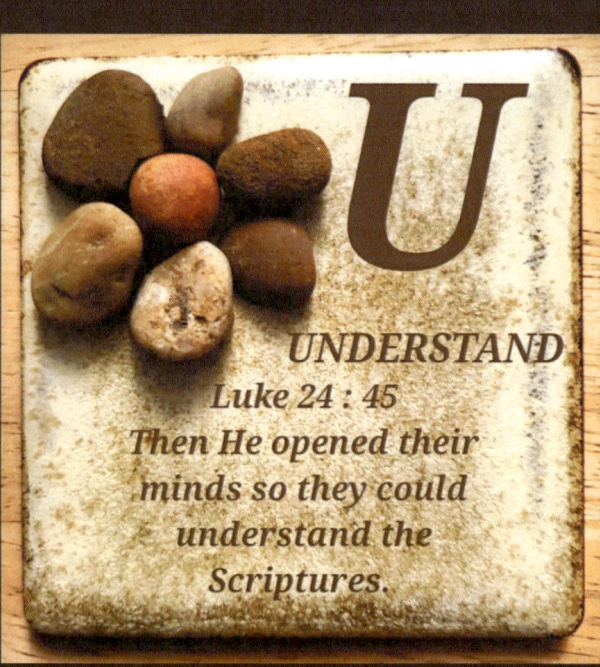

U

UNDERSTAND

Luke 24 : 45

Then He opened their minds so they could understand the Scriptures.

Lord Jesus,
Open my mind to understand
Scripture.
Open the eyes of my heart
to truly believe it!

VICTORIOUS

Psalm 20 : 5
We will shout for joy
when you are
victorious, and will lift
up our banners in the
Name of our God!

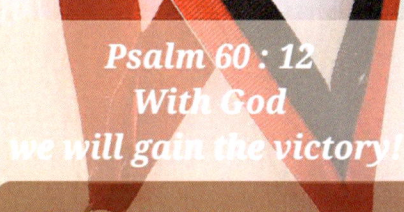

Psalm 60 : 12
With God
we will gain the victory!

Thank You Jesus for my victory!

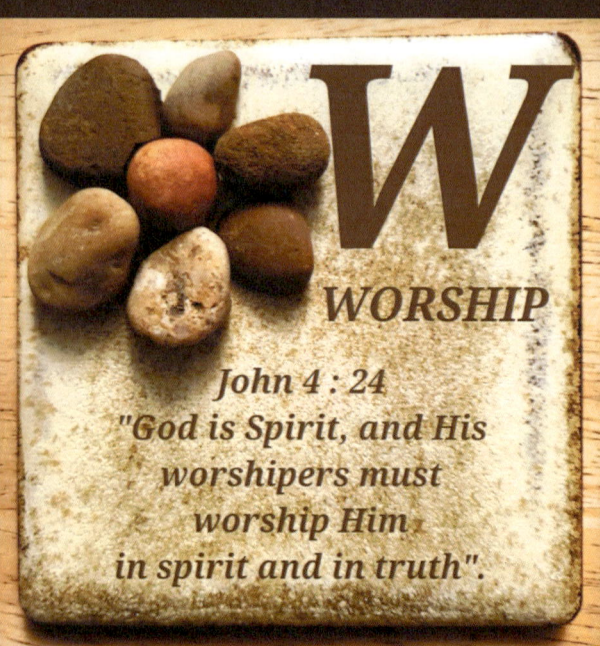

W

WORSHIP

John 4 : 24
"God is Spirit, and His
worshipers must
worship Him
in spirit and in truth".

Holy, Holy, Holy!

186

Reginald Heber   (Nicæa)   John B. Dykes

1. Ho-ly, ho-ly, ho-ly! Lord God Al-might-y! Ear-ly in the
morn-ing our song shall rise to Thee; Ho-ly, ho-ly, ho-ly!

2. Ho-ly, ho-ly, ho-ly! all the saints a-dore Thee, Cast-ing down their
gold-en crowns a-round the crys-tal sea; Cher-u-bim and ser-a-phim

3. Ho-ly, ho-ly, ho-ly! tho' the dark-ness hide Thee, Tho' the eye of
sin-ful man Thy glo-ry may not see; On-ly Thou art ho-ly!

4. Ho-ly, ho-ly, ho-ly! Lord God Al-might-y! All Thy works shall
praise Thy name, in earth, and sky, and sea; Ho-ly, ho-ly, ho-ly!

I worship You, my God

X

EXPECTATION

Romans 8 : 18, 19
I consider that the present
sufferings are not worth
comparing with the glory that will
be revealed in us! The creation
waits in eager expectation for the
sons of God to be
revealed!

Lord, I also wait in eager expectation for Your final plan to be revealed!

Y

"YES"

2 Corinthians 1 : 20
No matter how many
promises God has made,
they are "Yes" in Christ.

Lord, I say 'Yes' to You because You have said 'Yes' to me!

Z

ZEAL

Romans 12 : 11
*Never be lacking in zeal,
but keep your spiritual
fervor, serving the Lord.*

John 2 : 17
His disciples remembered
that it is written:
"Zeal for Your house
consumes Me".

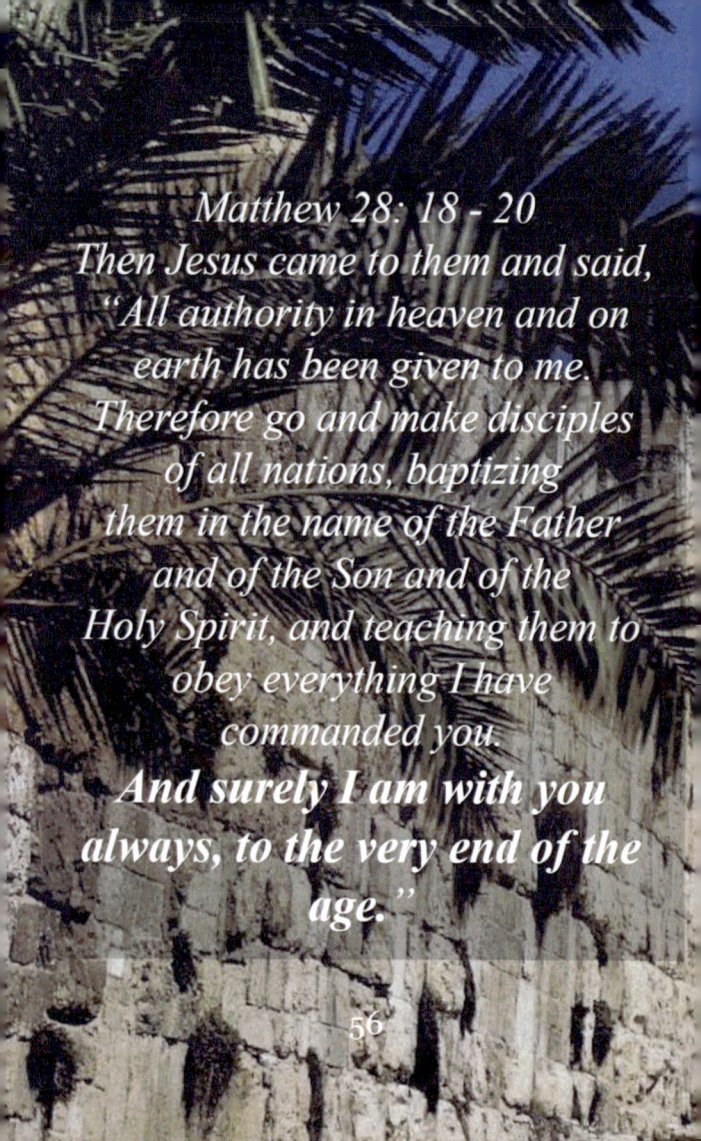

Matthew 28: 18 - 20
Then Jesus came to them and said,
"All authority in heaven and on
earth has been given to me.
Therefore go and make disciples
of all nations, baptizing
them in the name of the Father
and of the Son and of the
Holy Spirit, and teaching them to
obey everything I have
commanded you.
**And surely I am with you
always, to the very end of the
age."**

56

2 Thessalonians 2: 16 & 17

May our Lord Jesus Christ Himself and God our Father, who loved us and by His grace gave us eternal encouragement and good hope, encourage your hearts and strengthen you in every good deed and word.

Amen

More in the series!

We hope you found this inspirational
pocketbook uplifting. The simple
affirmative statements, illustrations,
and scriptures were prayerfully compiled
by the author to bring you
strength and peace.

Plus, there are more books in the series!
They'd make a beautiful gift for someone
you love. Available at select bookstores
and online. God bless!

*If you enjoyed this book, please consider
leaving a positive rating or review.*

www.ingramcontent.com/pod-product-compliance
Lightning Source LLC
Chambersburg PA
CBRC090835120626
46547CB00011B/697